WORDSWORTH'S DUDDON REVISITED

WORDSWORTH'S DUDDON REVISITED

Text by John Dawson
Photographs by David Briggs

CICERONE PRESS

MILNTHORPE, CUMBRIA, ENGLAND

*For Erica Briggs and to the memory of Thomas
Briggs O.B.E., who awakened my interest in
photography
and to the memory of Stanley and Mary Dawson,
who loved the valley.*

Acknowledgments

David Briggs wishes to thank:
his wife Jill and daughters Sarah and Jenny for
accepting his many absences in the Duddon and
darkroom,
all those Duddon folk for their friendliness and
accepting a photographer in their midst,
Jim Greenwood for his enthusiasm for these landscape
photographs and his readily given advice,
Gail, Alison and Leanne for practical help.

Printed in Great Britain at the University Printing House, Oxford
by David Stanford Printer to the University

Contents

The Duddon Sonnets

Although the River Duddon is not as closely identified in the public mind with Wordsworth as some other parts of the Lake District, this stream held a special place in his affection and esteem. Indeed, in his *'Guide to the Lakes'* he bestowed on it his highest praise, writing with respect to Lakeland rivers:

'The water is perfectly pellucid, through which many places are seen, to a great depth, their beds of rock, or of blue gravel, which gives to the water itself an exquisitely cerulean colour; this is particularly striking in the rivers Derwent and Duddon, which may be compared, such and so various are their beauties, to any two rivers of equal length of course in any country'.

Wordsworth's preferred approach to the Duddon valley was from Coniston over the Walna Scar road, in those days maintained along its full length in the interests both of local pedestrians going about their necessary business and industrial traffic, particularly associated with the wool trade and the slate quarries. His prose description of the scene as he descended towards the little side valley drained by Tarn Beck is a wonderful evocation of atmosphere in which the visible objects are fused with his own emotional response to what he saw. As he picked out the significant detail, Wordsworth composed a picture for the mind's eye, at the same time moulding our own ideal of earthly content through his own romantic dream:

'This recess, towards the close of September, when the after-grass of the meadows is still of a fresh green, with the leaves of many of the trees faded, but perhaps none fallen, is truly enchanting .... Russet and craggy hills, of bold and varied outline, surround the level valley, which is besprinkled with grey rocks plumed with birch trees. A few homesteads are interspersed, in some places peeping out from among the rocks like hermitages, whose site has been chosen for the benefit on the sunshine as well as shelter; in other instances, the dwelling house, barn and byre compose together a cruciform structure, which, with its embowering trees, and the ivy clothing part of the walls and roof like a fleece, call to mind the remains of an ancient abbey. Time, in most cases, and nature everywhere, have given a sanctity to the humble works of man, that are scattered over this peaceful retirement. Hence a harmony of tone and colour, a consummation and perfection of beauty, which would have been marred had aim or purpose interfered with the course of convenience, utility or necessity. This unvitiated region stands in no need of the veil of twilight to soften or disguise its features. As it glistens in the morning sunshine, it would fill the spectator's heart with gladsomeness.'

'Looking from our chosen station, he would feel an impatience to rove among its pathways, to be greeted by the milkmaid, to wander from house to house exchanging 'Good morrows' as he passed the open doors; but, at evening, when the sun is set, and a pearly light gleams from the western quarter of the sky, with an answering light from the smooth surface of the meadows; when the trees are dusky, but each kind still distinguishable; when the cool air had condensed the blue smoke rising from the cottage chimneys; when the dark mossy stones seem to sleep in the bed of the foaming brook; THEN he would be unwilling to move forward, not less from a reluctance to relinquish what he beholds, than from an apprehension of disturbing, by his approach, the quietness beneath him ...'

This timeless idyll was distilled from a lifetime's acquaintance with the Duddon and its valley. Wordsworth's earliest encounter with the river had been as a schoolboy. One day he went with a Hawkshead man to fish near the source of the Duddon. The day turned out a total disaster, and Wordsworth's shudders may still be felt in his account of the expedition, written years later:

'We fished a great part of the day with very sorry success, the rain pouring torrents, and long before we got home I was worn out with fatigue; and, if the good man had not carried me on his back, I must have lain down under the best shelter I could find. Little did I then think it would have been my lot to celebrate, in a strain of love and admiration, the stream which for many years I never thought of without recollections of disappointment and distress.'

Fortunately the weather was better when he revisited the Duddon during his long vacations from Cambridge. He used to stay with cousins who lived at Broughton-in-Furness, within comfortable walking distance of Ulpha or Seathwaite, and together they spent many happy days exploring the valley. He was back in 1794; then in 1811 he brought Mary here. Leaving the children to go in a pony cart, William and Mary travelled up the valley on foot. These, too, were happy days. 'I have many affecting remembrances (of Duddon),' he wrote later,'

...especially things that occurred on its banks during the later part of that visit to the seaside, of which the former part is detailed in my Epistle to Sir George Beaumont.'

It was from intimate personal experience, therefore, that Wordsworth settled down in late November 1818 to translate his love for Duddon into a series of sonnets. In a burst of creative activity he wrote 19 of the 34 poems which make up the cycle. Mary gives us a glimpse of the scene in a letter to Sara Hutchinson:

'William is sitting with his feet on the fender and his verses in his hand - nay now they have dropped upon his knees and he is asleep from sheer exhaustion - he has worked so long - he has written 21 sonnets (including two old ones) on the river Duddon - they all together compose one poem.'

The 'two old ones' are No.14 *(0 Mountain Stream)*, which had appeared in the *'Poems in Two Volumes'*, 1807; and No.26 *(Return, Content)* rewritten from a sonnet composed some time before 1804 - its original was one of the pieces transcribed for Coleridge when he went to Malta.

The remaining sonnets were written at intervals during 1819, so that it was possible to include the whole series in *'Miscellaneous Poems', Vol.III,* published in May 1820. Professor Wilson *(Christopher North)* at once gave them a very favourable review in *'Blackwood's Magazine'*, and Wordsworth himself seems to have been pleased by the public reception of the poems. Many years later, he said that these sonnets had been 'wonderfully popular', and 'more warmly received' than any of his other writings. Maybe the favourable reception was due to the fact that the poems are quite straightforward, and may be understood without difficulty by the ordinary reader. The tight discipline imposed by the sonnet form prevented the excessive diffuseness which afflicted *'The Excursion'*, and the precise geographical location discouraged either the difficult symbolism of *'The White Doe of Rylstone'*, or the oddity of *'Peter Bell'*. Readers can relate easily to the theme of a river running through a mountainous, then pastoral landscape on its journey to the sea, and can see the point of the historical references.

The theme, moreover, was probably one very close to Wordsworth's heart. In earlier years the river Wye at Tintern had appealed powerfully to his imagination, and the words written in 1798, a few miles above the abbey, could well be applied to his later mediations on the Duddon:

'O sylvan Wye: thou wandered through the woods:
How often has my spirit turned to thee:'

In the sonnets, the river gives a unity to the glimpses of the landscape through which it runs, a landscape glorious in itself, made yet more beautiful by the hand of many over many generations. Wordsworth appreciated this delicate balance, and as we read we can feel his awareness of the historical associations of each place. At the same time his own deep emotional response to the landscape prevents him from writing a conventional genteel-topographical account in the manner of, say, William Green.

The sequence begins at the source of the Duddon with an invocation that the verse may match the qualities of the stream it celebrates:

'Pure flow the verse, pure, vigorous, free and bright,
For Duddon, long-loved Duddon is my theme!'

The second and third sonnets described the high wilderness in which the river springs. The 'child of the clouds' emerges from a bed of brilliant moss set in the midst of a fearful desolation. But soon, in sonnet No.4, the tiny stream is rushing down the crags 'robed instantly in garb of snow-white foam'. Wrynose Bottom in those days was not uninhabited - Gaitscale, the last farm, was still occupied; so even before he reached Cockley Beck Wordsworth could begin to think of the trees and flowers that bordered the stream, the sheltering pines at an unidentifiable 'cottage rude and grey', the wild strawberry, eyebright and purple thyme, each in its season.

As in No.2, so in sonnet No.8 the poet's mind runs back to the ancient times, and now he tries to fathom the thoughts of the unknowable person first to sojourn here:

'What hopes came with him? What designs were spread
Along his path? ....
No voice replies.'

The stepping stones a little farther downstream, however, can bring a more lively response. The Duddon has now grown from a 'straggling rill' to a 'brook of loud and stately march'. Here, as the swift waters rush between the stones, the child can put his budding courage to the proof, the old man thinks - 'how fast time runs, life's end how near,' and the girl, too timid to advance, requires the outstretched hand of her swain to guide here from stone to stone across the dizzy flood.

But the hazards of the stepping stones are insignificant compared with the chasms the river has carved for itself, at Birk's Bridge, or through Wallowbarrow gorge. It is with feelings of joyful relief that the poet greets the more open, settled landscape around Seathwaite:

'Hail to the fields - with dwellings sprinked o'er!'

Here again Wordsworth falls to musing, but Seathwaite Chapel recalls him from the Roman legionaries bending the knee to Jove and Mars to Robert Walker of nearer and more precise fame. It might plausibly be argued that the entire sequence of poems is a memorial to 'Wonderful' Walker, for whom Wordsworth clearly had a profound respect: 'a gospel teacher ... whose good works formed an endless retinue.' He added a biographical essay of some 6,000 words in his later *'Notes'* to the sonnets, extolling Walker's virtues, thereby, perhaps, creating the legend that has clung to Walker ever since.

Sonnets 19 and 20 return to the more purely topographical, with a detour to Tarn beck, 'hurrying with lordly Duddon to unite', and then, - a calm pause in the endless rush of the waters - a look at the plain of Donnerdale, flowery enough to beautify even Elysium. Here the poet's gently melancholy reverie as he thinks of his earliest wanderings along these shores, is temporarily interrupted by the busy activity of the dalesmen. Dogs bark, boys and men shout, as the bleating sheep are driven into the waters for a dipping, prelude to the annual shearing. By afternoon all is quiet again; Wordsworth seeks a spot sheltered from the heat of the sun, and his thoughts turn to Mary, whose absence is the only flaw in the perfection of his retreat:

'... The waters seem to waste
Their vocal charm; their sparklings cease to please.'

At this point one wonders whether, at their deepest level, the poems are for Mary, recollections of shared experiences, especially that memorable expedition of 1811. Sonnet No.30 indeed oddly anticipates an unfortunate misadventure which befell in 1840 when William, Mary, Dora, their friend Isabella Fenwick and her niece, Edward Quillinan (the Wordsworths' future son-in-law) and Miss Quillinan made a carriage tour to the Duddon valley. Instead of walking on with the others beyond Seathwaite, Mary said she would go back towards Ulpha. 'But,' wrote Wordsworth, in his *'Notes'* to the sonnets,

'she was tempted out of the main road to ascend a rocky eminence near it, thinking it impossible we should pass without seeing her. This, however, unfortunately happened, and then ensued vexation and distress, especially to me, which I should have been ashamed to have recorded, for I lost my temper entirely.'

Quillinan went back from Ulpha in one of the carriages; he met Mary on the road, and took her back to Broughton, where the whole party was 'reunited, and spent a happy evening'. But clearly William had been most upset by the thought that Mary might have had some accident.

'Neither I nor those that were with me,' he continued, 'saw her again till we reached the inn at Broughton, 7 miles. This may perhaps excuse my irritability on the occasion, for I could not but think she had been much to blame. It appeared, however, on explanation, that she had remained on the rock (a point above the road to which she had climbed) calling out and waving her handkerchief as we were passing, in order that we also might ascend, and enjoy a prospect which had much charmed her.'

The incident, trivial enough in itself, reveals in Wordsworth's unreasonable irritability the depth of his concern for Mary.

Returning to the proper order of the sonnets, the prevailing mood of melancholy is continued in these reaches where Duddon has come to maturity. Some of the friends of childhood days are gone; the old hall which looks down to the valley is 'fallen, and diffused into a shapeless heap'. It is time to go:

'I rose while yet the cattle, heat-opprest,
Crowded together under rustling trees,
Brushed by the current of the water breeze..'

Sonnet No.29, as we continue the journey, is generally supposed to refer to the old Quaker burial ground, high on the fellside, away from the modern road, yet its martial imagery does not seem to match the folk who lie there. In No.31, however, we are quite definitely in Ulpha churchyard. Calm and serene, the little church has been the embodiment of eternal truths for each succeeding generation of dalesfolk, where

'..distant moonlit mountains faintly shine
Soothed by the unseen river's gentle roar.'

Below Ulpha bridge the river enters its last reach before the sea, broader now, but not less rocky or flower-garlanded than in its earlier course. Wordsworth did not relate any sonnets specifically to this section. Maybe he felt that anything else would be an anti-climax after the Kirk of Ulpha, so the reader is transported directly to the estuary:

'Majestic Duddon, over smooth flat sands
Gliding in silence with unfettered sweep.'

Duddon has come to the end of its journey, where even the mightiest rivers sink into powerless sleep; and so the poet inevitably reflects on his own journey through life, a comparison that has never been far below the surface throughout the sequence:

'And may thy poet, cloud-born stream, be free in peace of heart, in calm
   of mind,
And soul, to mingle with eternity!'

In the valedictory sonnet Wordsworth moves from a personal to a universal note and presents Duddon as a symbol of all that is permanent -

'Still glides the stream, and shall not cease to glide' -

before his final dignified acceptance of mortality.

WORDSWORTH'S DUDDON SONNETS

RIVER DUDDON

I.

NOT envying shades which haply yet may throw
A grateful coolness round that rocky spring,
Blandusia, once responsive to the string
Of the Horatian lyre with babbling flow;
Careless of flowers that in perennial blow
Round the moist marge of Persian fountains cling;
Heedless of Alpine torrents thundering
Through icy portals radiant as heaven's bow;
I seek the birthplace of a native stream.
All hail, ye mountains! hail, thou morning light!
Better to breathe upon this aery height
Than pass in needless sleep from dream to dream:
pure flow the verse, pure, vigorous, free, and bright,
For Duddon, long-loved Duddon is my theme!

A grateful coolness round that rocky spring

II

CHILD of the clouds! remote from every taint
Of sordid industry thy lot is cast;
Thine are the honours of the lofty waste;
Not seldom, when with heat the valleys faint,
Thy hand-maid frost with spangled tissue quaint
Thy cradle decks; to chant thy birth thou hast
No meaner poet than the whistling blast,
And desolation is thy patron-saint!
She guards thee, ruthless power! who would not spare
Those mighty forests, once the bison's screen,
Where stalked the huge deer to his shaggy lair
Through paths and alleys roofed with sombre green,
Thousands of years before the silent air
Was pierced by whizzing shaft of hunter keen!

Thy hand-maid frost with spangled tissue quaint

III

HOW shall I paint thee? – Be this naked stone
My seat while I give way to such intent;
Pleased could my verse, a speaking monument,
Make to the eyes of men they features known
But as of all those tripping lambs not one
Outruns his fellows, so hath nature lent
To thy beginning naught that doth present
Peculiar grounds for hope to build upon.
To dignify the spot that gives thee birth,
No sign of hoar antiquity's esteem
Appears, and none of modern fortune's care;
Yet thou thyself hast round thee shed a gleam
Of brilliant moss, instinct with freshness rare;
Prompt offering to they foster-mother earth

How shall I paint thee? - Be this naked stone
My seat while I give way to such intent

IV

TAKE, cradled nursling of the mountain, take
This parting glance, no negligent adieu!
A Protean change seems wrought while I pursue
The curves, a loosely-scattered chain doth make;
Or rather thou appear'st a glistering snake,
Silent, and to the gazer's eye untrue,
Thridding with sinuous lapse the rushes, through
Dwarf willows gliding, and by ferny brake.
Starts from a dizzy steep the undaunted rill
Robed instantly in garb of snow-white foam;
And laughing dares the adventurer, who hath clomb
So high, a rival purpose to fulfil;
Else let the dastard backward wend, and roam,
Seeking less bold achievement, where he will!

Starts from a dizzy steep the undaunted rill
Robed instantly in garb of snow-white foam

V

SOLE listener, Duddon! to the breeze that played
With thy clear voice, I caught the fitful sound
Wafted o'er sullen moss and craggy mound,
Unfruitful solitudes, that seemed to upbraid
The sun in heaven! – but now, to form a shade
For thee, green alders have together wound
Their foliage; ashes flung their arms around;
And birch-trees risen in silver colonnade.
And thou hast also tempted here to rise,
'Mid sheltering pines, this cottage rude and grey;
Whose ruddy children, by the mother's eyes
Carelessly watched, sport through the summer day,
Thy pleased associates – light as endless May
On infant bosoms lonely nature lies.

And birch trees risen in silver colonnade

VI

FLOWERS

ERE yet our course was graced with social trees
It lacked not old remains of hawthorn bowers,
Where small birds warbled to their paramours;
And, earlier still, was heard the hum of bees;
I saw them ply their harmless robberies,
And caught the fragrance which the sundry flowers,
Fed by the stream with soft perpetual showers
Plenteously yielded to the vagrant breeze.
There bloomed the strawberry of the wilderness;
The trembling eyebright showed her sapphire blue,
The thyme her purple, like the blush of even;
And, if the breath of some to no caress
Invited, forth they peeped so fair to view,
All kinds alike seemed favourites of Heaven.

It lacked not old remains of hawthorn bowers

VII

"CHANGE me, some god, into that breathing rose!"
The love-sick stripling fancifully sighs,
The envied flower, beholding, as it lies
On Laura's breast, in exquisite repose;
Or he would pass into her bird, that throws
The darts of song from out its wiry cage;
Enraptured, – could he for himself engage
The thousandth part of what the nymph bestows,
And what the little careless innocent
Ungraciously receives Too daring choice!
There are whose calmer mind it would content
To be an unculled floweret of the glen,
Fearless of plough and scythe; or darkling wren,
That tunes on Duddon's banks her slender voice.

That tunes on Duddon's banks her slender voice

VIII

WHAT aspect bore the man who roved or fled.
First of his tribe, to this dark dell – who first
In this pellucid current slaked his thirst?
What hopes came with him? what designs were spread
Along his path? His unprotected bed
What dreams encompassed? Was the intruder nursed
In hideous usages, and rites accursed,
That thinned the living and disturbed the dead?
No voice replies; – the earth, the air is mute;
And thou, blue streamlet, murmuring yield'st no more
Than a soft record that whatever fruit
Of ignorance thou mightst witness heretofore,
Thy function was to heal and to restore,
To soothe and cleanse, not madden and pollute!

First of his tribe, to this dark dell

IX
THE STEPPING—STONES

THE struggling rill insensibly is grown
Into a brook of loud and stately march,
Crossed ever and anon by plank and arch;
And, for like use, lo! what might seem a zone
Chosen for ornament: stone matched with stone
In studied symmetry, with interspace
For the clear waters to pursue their race
Without restraint. – How swiftly have they flown,
Succeeding – still succeeding! Here the child
Puts, when the high—swoln flood runs fierce and wild,
His budding courage to the proof; — and here
Declining manhood learns to note the sly
And sure encroachments of infirmity,
Thinking how fast time runs, life's end how near!

X

NOT so that pair whose youthful spirits dance
With prompt emotion, urging them to pass;
A sweet confusion checks the shepherd-lass;
Blushing she eyes the dizzy flood askance, –
To stop ashamed – too timid to advance;
She ventures once again – another pause!
His outstretched hand he tauntingly withdraws –
She sues for help with piteous utterance!
Chidden she chides again; the thrilling touch
Both feel when he renews the wished-for aid:
Ah! if their fluttering hearts should stir too much
Should beat too strongly, both may be betrayed.
The frolic loves who, from yon high rock, see
The struggle, clap their wings for victory!

Chosen for ornament: stone matched with stone
In studied symmetry, with interspace
For the clear waters to pursue their race

XI

THE FAERY CHASM

NO fiction was it of the antique age;
A sky-blue stone, within this sunless cleft,
Is of the very footmarks unbereft
Which tiny elves impressed; on that smooth stage
Dancing with all their brilliant equipage
In secret revels – haply after theft
Of some sweet babe, flower stolen, and coarse weed left
For the distracted mother to assuage
Her grief with, as she might! – But, where, oh! where
Is traceable a Vestige of the notes
That ruled those dances, wild in character?
Deep underground? – Or in the upper air,
On the shrill wind of midnight? or where floats
O'er twilight fields the autumnal gossamer?

A sky-blue stone, within this sunless cleft

XII

HINTS FOR THE FANCY

ON, loitering muse – the swift stream chides us – on!
Albeit his deep-worn channel doth immure
Objects immense portrayed in miniature,
Wild shapes for many a strange comparison!
Niagaras, Alpine passes, and anon
Abodes of Naiads, calm abysses pure,
Bright liquid mansions, fashioned to endure
When the broad oak drops, a leafless skeleton
And the solidities of mortal pride,
Palace and tower, are crumbled into dust!
The bard who walks with Duddon for his guide,
Shall find such toys of fancy thickly set; –
Turn from the sight, enamoured muse – we must;
And, if thou canst, leave them without regret!

Bright liquid mansions, fashioned to endure

XIII

OPEN PROSPECT

HAIL to the fields − with dwellings sprinkled o'er,
And one small hamlet, under a green hill,
Clustered with barn and byre, and spouting mill!
A glance suffices; − should we wish for more,
Gay June would scorn us: but when bleak winds roar
Through the stiff lance-like shoots of pollard ash,
Dread swell of sound! loud as the gusts that lash
The matted forests of Ontario's shore
By wasteful steel unsmitten, then would I
Turn into port, − and, reckless of the gale.
Reckless of angry Duddon sweeping by.
While the warm hearth exalts the mantling ale,
Laugh with the generous household heartily
At all the merry pranks of Donnerdale!

Hail to the fields - with dwellings sprinkled o'er,
And one small hamlet, under a green hill

XIV

O MOUNTAIN stream! the shepherd and his cot
Are privileged inmates of deep solitude;
Nor would the nicest anchorite exclude
A field or two of brighter green, or plot
Of tillage-ground, that seemeth like a spot
Of stationary sunshine: – thou hast viewed
These only, Duddon! with their paths renewed
By fits and starts, yet this contents thee not.
Thee hath some awful spirit impelled to leave,
Utterly to desert, the haunts of men,
Though simple thy companions were and few;
And through this wilderness a passage cleave
Attended but by thy own voice, save when
The clouds and fowls of the air thy way pursue!

And through this wilderness, a passage cleave

XV

FROM this deep chasm – where quivering sunbeams play
Upon its loftiest crags – mine eyes behold
A gloomy niche, capacious, blank, and cold;
A concave free from shrubs and mosses gray;
In semblance fresh, as if, with dire affray,
Some statue, placed amid these regions old
For tutelary service, thence had rolled,
Startling the flight of timid yesterday!
Was it by mortals sculptured? – weary slaves
Of slow endeavour! or abruptly cast
Into rude shape by fire, with roaring blast
Tempestuously let loose from central caves?
Or fashioned by the turbulence of waves,
Then, when o'er highest hills the deluge past?

XVI
AMERICAN TRADITION

SUCH fruitless questions may not long beguile
Or plague the fancy, 'mid the sculptured shows
Conspicuous yet where Oroonoko flows;
There would the Indian answer with a smile
Aimed at the white man's ignorance, the while
Of the Great Waters telling how they rose,
Covered the plains, and, wandering where they chose,
Mounted through every intricate defile,
Triumphant. – Inundation wide and deep
O'er which his fathers urged, to ridge and steep
Else unapproachable, their buoyant way;
And carved, on mural cliff's undreaded side,
Sun, moon, and stars, and beast of chase or prey;
Whate'er they sought, shunned, loved, or deified!

Then, when o'er highest hills the deluge past?

XVII

RETURN

A DARK plume fetch me from yon blasted yew,
Perched on whose top the Danish raven croaks;
Aloft, the imperial bird of Rome invokes
Departed ages, shedding where he flew
Loose fragments of wild wailing, that bestrew
The clouds, and thrill the chambers of the rocks,
And into silence hush the timorous flocks,
That, calmly couching while the nightly dew
Moistened each fleece, beneath the twinkling stars
Slept amid that lone camp on Hardknot's height,
Whose guardians bent the knee to Jove and Mars:
Or, near that mystic round of Druid frame
Tardily sinking by its proper weight
Deep into patient earth, from whose smooth breast it
came!

And into silence hush the timorous flocks

XVIII

SEATHWAITE CHAPEL

SACRED religion, "mother of form and fear,"
Dread arbitress of mutable respect.
New rites ordaining, when the old are wrecked,
Or crease to please the fickle worshipper;
If one strong wish may be embosomed here,
Mother of love! for this deep vale, protect
Truth's holy lamp, pure source of bright effect,
Gifted to purge the vapoury atmosphere
That seeks to stifle it; – as in those days
When this low pile a gospel teacher knew,
Whose good works formed an endless retinue:
Such priest as Chaucer sang in fervent lays;
Such as the Heaven-taught skill of Herbert drew;
And tender Goldsmith crowned with deathless praise!

When this low pile a gospel teacher knew,
Whose good works formed an endless retinue

XIX

TRIBUTARY STREAM

MY frame hath often trembled with delight
When hope presented some far-distant good,
That seemed from Heaven descending, like the flood
Of yon pure waters, from their aery height
Hurrying with lordly Duddon to unite;
Who, 'mid a world of images imprest
On the calm depth of his transparent breast,
Appears to cherish most that torrent white,
The fairest, softest, liveliest of them all!
And seldom hath ear listened to a tune
More lulling than the busy hum of noon,
Swoln by that voice – whose murmur musical
Announces to the thirsty fields a boon
Dewy and fresh, till showers again shall fall.

Of yon pure waters, from their aery height
Hurrying with lordly Duddon to unite

XX

THE PLAIN OF DONNERDALE

THE old inventive poets, had they seen,
Or ratherfelt, the entrancement that detains
Thy waters, Duddon! 'mid these flowery plains,
The still repose, the liquid lapse serene,
Transferred to bowers imperishably green,
Had beautified Elysium! But these chains
Will soon be broken; — a rough course remains,
Rough as the past; where thou, of placid mien,
Innocuous as a firstling of the flock,
And countenanced like a soft cerulean sky,
Shalt change thy temper; and, with many a shock
Given and received in mutual jeopardy,
Dance like a Bacchanal, from rock to rock,
Tossing her frantic thyrsus wide and high!

Thy waters, Duddon! 'mid these flowery plains

XXI

WHENCE that low voice? – A whisper from the heart,
That told of days long past, when here I roved
With friends and kindred tenderly beloved;
Some who had early mandates to depart,
Yet are allowed to steal my path athwart
By Duddon's side; once more do we unite,
Once more beneath the kind earth's tranquil light;
And smothered joys into new being start.
From her unworthy seat, the cloudy stall
Of time, breaks forth triumphant Memory;
Her glistening tresses bound, yet light and free
As golden locks of birch, that rise and fall
On gales that breathe too gently to recal
Aught of the fading year's inclemency!

Once more beneath the kind earth's tranquil light

XXII

TRADITION

A LOVE-LORN maid, at some far-distant time,
Came to this hidden pool, whose depths surpass
In crystal clearness Dian's looking-glass;
And, gazing, saw that rose, which from the prime
Derives its name, reflected as the chime
Of echo doth reverberate some sweet sound:
The starry treasure from the blue profound
She longed to ravish; – shall she plunge, or climb
The humid precipice, and seize the guest
Of April, smiling high in upper air?
Desperate alternative! what fiend could dare
To prompt the thought? – Upon the steep rock's breast
The lonely primrose yet renews its bloom,
Untouched memento of her hapless doom!

Came to this hidden pool, whose depths surpass
In crystal clearness Dian's looking-glass

XXIII

SHEEP-WASHING

SAD thoughts, avaunt! – the favour of the year,
Poured on the fleece-encumbered flock, invites
To laving currents, for prelusive rites
Duly performed before the dalesmen shear
Their panting charge. The distant mountains hear,
Hear and repeat, the turmoil that unites
Clamour of boys with innocent despites
Of barking dogs, and bleatings from strange fear.
Meanwhile, if Duddon's spotless breast receive
Unwelcome mixtures as the uncouth noise
Thickens, the pastoral river will forgive
Such wrong; nor need we blame the licensed joys,
Though false to nature's quiet equipoise:
Frank are the sports, the stains are fugitive.

Of barking dogs, and bleatings from strange fear

XXIV

THE RESTING-PLACE

MID-NOON is past; – upon the sultry mead
No zephyr breathes, no cloud its shadow throws:
If we advance unstrengthened by repose,
Farewell the solace of the fragrant reed!
This nook, with woodbine hung and straggling weed,
Tempting recess as ever pilgrim chose,
Half grot, half arbour, proffers to inclose
Body and mind from molestation freed,
In narrow compass – narrow as itself:
Or if the fancy, too industrious elf,
Be loth that we should breathe a while exempt
From new incitements friendly to our task,
There wants not stealthy prospect, that may tempt
Loose idless to forego our wily mask.

Mid-noon is past; - upon the sultry mead
No zephyr breathes, no cloud its shadow throws

XXV

METHINKS 'twere no unprecedented feat
Should some benignant minister of air
Lift, and incircle with a cloudy chair,
The one for whom my heart shall ever beat
With tenderest love' – or, if a safer seat
Atween his downy wings be furnished, there
Would lodge her, and the cherished burden bear
O'er hill and valley to this dim retreat!
Rough ways my steps have trod; too rough and long
For her companionship; here dwells soft ease:
With sweets which she partakes not some distaste
Mingles, and lurking consciousness of wrong;
Languish the flowers; the waters seem to waste
Their vocal charm; their sparklings cease to please.

Rough ways my steps have trod; too rough and long

XXVI

RETURN, content! for fondly I pursued,
Even when a child, the streams – unheard, unseen;
Through tangled woods, impending rocks between;
Or, free as air, with flying inquest viewed
The sullen reservoirs whence their bold brood,
Pure as the morning, fretful, boisterous keen,
Green as the salt-sea billows, white and green,
Poured down the hills, a choral multitude!
Nor have I tracked their course for scanty gains;
They taught me random cares and truant joys,
That shield from mischief and preserve from stains
Vague minds, while men are growing out of boys;
Maturer fancy owes to their rough noise
Impetuous thoughts that brook not servile reins.

Through tangled woods, impending rocks between

XXVII

FALLEN, and diffused into a shapeless heap,
Or quietly self-buried in earth's mould,
Is that embattled house, whose massy keep
Flung from yon cliff a shadow large and cold. –
There dwelt the gay, the bountiful, the bold,
Till nightly lamentations, like the sweep
Of winds – though winds were silent, struck a deep
And lasting terror through that ancient hold.
Its line of warriors fled; – they shrunk when tried
By ghostly power: – but Time's unsparing hand
Hath plucked such foes, like weeds, from out the land;
And now, if men with men in peace abide,
All other strength the weakest may withstand,
All worse assaults may safely be defied.

Is that embattled house, whose massy keep
Flung from yon cliff a shadow large and cold

XXVIII.

JOURNEY RENEWED

I ROSE while yet the cattle, heat-opprest,
Crowded together under rustling trees,
Brushed by the current of the water-breeze;
And for their sakes, and love of all that rest,
On Duddon's margin, in the sheltering nest;
For all the startled scaly tribes that slink
Into his coverts, and each fearless link
Of dancing insects forged upon his breast;
For these, and hopes and recollections worn
Close to the vital seat of human clay;
Glad meetings, – tender partings – that upstay
The drooping mind of absence, by vows sworn
In his pure presence near the trysting thorn;
I thanked the leader of my onward way.

I rose while yet the cattle, heat opprest,
Crowded together under rustling trees

XXIX

NO record tells of lance opposed to lance,
Horse charging horse, 'mid these retired domains;
Tells that their turf drank purple from the veins
Of heroes fallen, or struggling to advance,
Till doubtful combat issued in a trance
Of victory, that struck through heart and reins,
Even to the inmost seat of mortal plains,
and lightened o'er the pallid countenance.
Yet, to the loyal and the brave, who lie
In the black earth, neglected and forlorn,
The passing winds memorial tribute pay;
The torrents chant their praise, inspiring scorn
Of power unsurped with proclamation high,
And glad acknowledgement of lawful sway.

Yet to the loyal and the brave, who lie
In the black earth, neglected and forlorn

XXX.

WHO swerves from innocence, who makes divorce
Of that serene companion – a good name,
Recovers not his loss; but walks with shame,
With doubt, with fear, and haply with remorse.
And oft-times he, who, yielding to the force
Of chance temptation, ere his journey end,
From chosen comrade turns, or faithful friend,
In vain shall rue the broken intercourse.
Not so with such as loosely wear the chain
That binds them, pleasant river! to thy side: –
Through the rough copse wheel thou with hasty stride,
I choose to saunter o'er the grassy plain,
Sure, when the separation has been tried,
That we, who part in love, shall meet again.

I choose to saunter o'er the grassy plain

XXXI

THE Kirk of Ulpha to the pilgrim's eye
Is welcome as a star, that doth present
Its shining forehead through the peaceful rent
Of a black cloud diffused o'er half the sky:
Or as a fruitful palm-tree towering high
O'er the parched waste beside an Arab's tent;
Or the Indian tree whose branches, downward bent,
Take root again, a boundless canopy.
How sweet were leisure! could it yield no more
Than 'mid that wave-washed churchyard to recline,
From pastoral graves extracting thoughts devine;
Or there to pace, and mark the summits hoar
Of distant moon-lit mountains faintly shine,
Soothed by the unseen river's gentle roar.

The Kirk of Ulpha to the pilgrim's eye
is welcome as a star

XXXII.

NOT hurled precipitous from steep to steep;
Lingering no more 'mid flower-enamelled lands
And blooming thickets; nor by rocky bands
Held; – but in radiant progress toward the deep
Where mightiest rivers into powerless sleep
Sink, and forget their nature; – now expands
Majestic Duddon, over smooth flat sands
Gliding in silence with unfettered sweep!
Beneath an ampler sky a region wide
Is opened round him: – hamlets, towers, and towns,
And blue-topped hills, behold him from afar;
In stately mien to sovereign Thames allied
Spreading his bosom under Kentish downs,
With commerce freighted, or triumphant war.

Majestic Duddon, over smooth flat sands
Gliding in silence with unfettered sweep!

XXXIII
CONCLUSION

BUT here no cannon thunders to the gale;
Upon the wave no haughty pendants cast
A crimson splendour; lowly is the mast
That rises here, and humbly spread the sail;
While, less disturbed than in the narrow vale
Through which with strange vicissitudes he passed,
The wanderer seeks that receptacle vast
Where all his unambitious functions fail.
And may thy poet, cloud-borne stream! be free,
The sweets of earth contentedly resigned,
And each tumultuous working left behind
At seemly distance, to advance like thee,
Prepared, in peace of heart, in calm of mind
And soul, to mingle with eternity!

XXXIV
AFTER-THOUGHT

I THOUGHT of thee, my partner and my guide,
As being past away. Vain sympathies!
For, backward, Duddon! as I cast my eyes,
I see what was, and is, and will abide;
Still glides the stream, and shall not cease to glide;
The form remains, the function never dies;
While we, the brave, the mighty, and the wise,
We men, who in our morn of youth defied
The elements, must vanish; – be it so!
Enough, if something from our hands have power
To live, and act, and serve the future hour;
And if, as toward the silent tomb we go,
Through love, through hope, and faith's transcendant
dower,
We feel that we are greater than we know.

Still glides the stream, and shall not cease to glide

DUDDON
REVISITED

ESTUARY

Duddon sands are lonely, wide and windswept. No one goes there except fishermen and wildfowlers. When the late afternoon sunshine slants over the shoulder of Black Combe, it creates a world of bright dancing patterns on sand and water. A flock of oystercatchers rushes by, in close formation, their wild cries somehow magnified by the surrounding silence; or, in winter, a skein of wild geese stretches across the sky, heard before it is seen. The foaming river which Wordsworth followed from its source has been transformed into a series of shifting channels in the sand.

In wintertime the snow which blocks the passes at the head of the valley pursues the river along its entire course, so that the saltings become uninhabitable even for the sheep which at kinder seasons can be seen nibbling the grass. Today the farmers are the only folk whose business takes them regularly over this land. The cocklers whose harvest was once famous throughout the North-west have gone; the iron mines at Millom have been closed; and now none of the little ships whose sails Wordsworth saw come into the estuary to give scale and life to the surrounding emptiness.

Duddon Estuary, Black Combe and Foxfield

Duddon Estuary - snow and rushes

Duddon Estuary - Foxfield

DUDDON BRIDGE IRON FURNACE

The furnace has been silent and empty for many years. In its heyday two centuries ago a water wheel by the side of the building operated the great bellows situated opposite the furnace mouth. Men would be wheeling barrow loads of ore, flux and charcoal from the huge storehouses glimpsed at the rear. Their busy activity would be audible from far away – the sound of men and their pack horses at the unloading bays of the charcoal store, of ore being shovelled into barrows, the hum of the water wheel and the regular thump of the bellows. The local supply of charcoal was so abundant that the furnace continued in operation long after Abraham Darby had begun the change to coal.

In more recent times the site became completely derelict, but conservation work has now consolidated the buildings and driven back the relentlessly encroaching woodland. Once more it is possible to appreciate the scale of this industrial enterprise; the contrast with the present agricultural character of the Duddon valley is striking.

Duddon Bridge Iron Furnace

Duddon Bridge Iron Furnace - grasses

Duddon Bridge Iron Furnace -
View from charcoal store to furnace

DUDDON HALL

Not far above Duddon bridge, Duddon Hall stands on a platform of level ground overlooking the river. Once it was known as Whae House, but when Major John Cooper had the place rebuilt and gentrified at the turn of the 18th century, the name was changed to Duddon Hall. Its most unusual features are a well preserved ice-house down near the river, and the 'Temple,' a folly which was supposed to do duty as a chapel. The handsome stag surmounting its well proportional classical pediment gives some idea of the kind of god most honoured by worshippers there. Tradition has it that Cooper and his friends were devotees of cockfighting. When they held a mains at the Hall, they simply rearranged the pews in the chapel, and settled to an exciting session of slaughter and gaming. The atmosphere of a way of life now vanished hangs heavily about the buildings as they decay quietly and elegantly, inhabited only by the ghosts that haunted their stairs and corridors to startle many an unsuspecting Victorian visitor.

Duddon Hall Chapel

DUDDON HALL TO ULPHA

Between Duddon Hall and Ulpha the wide river dominates the scene. The farms are strung in a line above the valley floor, except where the land is too rough for cultivation of any kind. One such stretch between Stonestar and Sella has become a popular stopping place for picnicking and paddling visitors. Sella has been associated with the Cassons, one of the principal families of the area, for many generations. In many respects it is typical of the valley farms. Its land consists of the lower-lying fields, from which it is usually possible to make hay, and which provides good pasture, and the much greater area of upland grazing where the sheep flock spends its summer. From this higher ground brackens can be cut for bedding the cattle in winter, and peats dug for fuel. In the old days Sella was noted also for its fishing. Those were the times when the slate flags on the floors of the farm kitchens could not be seen for the fish laid out on them, when salmon had been taken for salting. Mrs Kirkby would not appreciate that sort of confusion all over the floor today. The spotless farm house is a wonderful blend of the traditional with the more up-to-date. Mr Kirkby can be seen with a favourite terrier enjoying a well-earned five minutes before going out to an afternoon's work among the sheep high on the fellside.

River Duddon between Duddon Hall and Ulpha

Barn and trees, Sella Farm

Farmer Kirby, Sella Farm

ULPHA

Ulpha is a scattered settlement in the lower part of the valley where the road which has come up from Duddon bridge on the Lancashire side crosses the river, and meets the road which has come down past the old Bobbin mill from South-west Cumberland. Higher up this road is Old Hall, a mediaeval stronghold of the Huddlestone family, Lords of Millom, who were also responsible for building Frith Hall as a hunting lodge in the early 17th century, some distance across the fields from Old Hall. Today the ruins of Frith Hall make a romantic silhouette against the sky when seen from Ulpha, and have given rise to numbers of fanciful tales. In Wordsworth's time Frith Hall was a farm house, and Old Hall had already fallen into decay.

But the ancient church is still the focal point both of the landscape and the community which has remained coherent and lively through the changing social patterns of the centuries. The Huddlestones have gone but the farmers are still there, and the tourist industry, in its different forms, has taken the place of the old woodland industries and the quarries.

Ulpha Church

Ulpha Post Office

Jobbie Youdell, Road Lengthsman

ULPHA SCHOOL

A village without a school is a village without a future. In the Duddon valley they have had to fight hard against the organization men who think only in terms of cost/efficiency. How could anyone with the least spark of imagination or sensitivity think of closing the school in a place like this? Here each child can develop as its talents and abilities are nurtured, and education can take on its real meaning. Pupils, parents and staff are a single caring community and in consequence the children don't relegate school to a separate, perhaps rather unpleasant compartment in their lives. Experiences come together, so that when they draw a picture to illustrate a poem or a scripture lesson, you may be pretty sure to find a line of fells in the background, decorated with spruce trees, and with a few sheep dotted around. The boys play in the finest school playground in the kingdom – but from their attitudes they could equally well be in the middle of an official nature study lesson. And what a great thing to be able to dance round a tree like this – these girls could easily be taking part in a physical education lesson. Many of the children will have to leave the valley when the time comes to find their work in life, but they will take with them the memory of an idyllic childhood.

Ulpha School - Grace Craig reading a story

Ulpha School - Children's playtime (girls)

Ulpha School - Children's playtime (boys)

DUDDON VALLEY SPORTS

The children figure largely in the annual Duddon Valley Sports. The grown ups have got the field ready – parents and others whom the children will know. In a place like this everyone is Somebody – not just an anonymous figure in a city street. And the grown ups come to the sports, too – a person can have an enjoyable afternoon without paying too much attention to the races. The whole programme is as far as can be imagined from manic athleticism of a typical school sports, never mind an AAA meeting. With luck, the grass will have been mown for hay not long previously, and the cattle will not have had opportunity to leave cowpats on the track. The events themselves retain the pleasant flavour of days when occasions like this were fun for everyone – skipping, and three-legged races. The prestige event of the valley sports is always the fell race; the youngsters make light of the ascent, then come bounding down in long sure-footed strides. To round off the afternoon the grown ups have been busy again – there are always mounds of cakes and sandwiches, and cups of tea and pop, more than the assembled company can possibly eat.

Duddon Valley Sports -
Locals enjoying a yarn while the children race

Duddon Valley Sports - Three legged race next

Duddon Valley Sports - Skipping race

SOCIAL EVENTS AT ULPHA

Social events are not only for the benefit of the children. The W.I. Flower Show is a good example of the serious side of life in the valley. Entering items for the Show brings everyone together, with no distinctions of occupation, age or social class. People go to a lot of trouble over their entries, which reflect the high standards of domestic management still taken for granted here. The judges are always knowledgeable outsiders, whose expertise everyone respects. This considerably reduces the risk of a show being a divisive influence, because anyone who carps afterwards at a decision is regarded as chewing on sour old grapes. All the same, there is a melancholy pleasure in disagreeing violently that one's own jam has only been placed third, or has even been left unmarked. Clearly, the judge, however skilled in soft fruit, however shiny her W.I. halo, is a tyro or a fool when it comes to assessing plum jam. Then there are produce stalls, and cups of tea. Nothing spectacular here; nothing of the wild rush of the urban jumble sale. There is time to assess the goods on show, to consider whether at only 3p cheaper than the supermarket price, something is worth carrying home; to speculate whether it was Auntie Mary who bought that rather rusty tin of soup. The tea and sandwiches are a blessing for the men, who have usually come only out of politeness. At least they can take the weight off their feet and make small talk until the ladies are through with the serious work.

WI Flower Show - judging the rum butter

WI Flower Show - produce stall

WI Flower Show - tea and cakes

ULPHA TO HALL DUNNERDALE

Walk up the valley from Ulpha, and you are never far from the river. Its waters tumble over the rocks in foaming cascades; the noise of the rapids is seldom still. Here and there a dark pool is betrayed by the PRIVATE notices that have been fixed to the trees in the hope of discouraging unlicensed fishermen. Rocky steps come marching down the fellsides to hem in the little green fields in the valley bottom. It is as if the fields have been forcibly wrenched away from the stony wilderness, and the boulders, cleared with infinite pains, used to make the walls behind which the lambs can shelter during springtime storms. A walk along the lane which leads to Kiln Bank before climbing out of the valley over Hoses should be a chastening experience for anyone who imagines that the Duddon landscape is just a pretty background for a touring holiday. Some of the field walls are higher than a man, and constructed of immense boulders that would need a substantial block and tackle to heave them into position. These boulders, cobbles they are called, still lie scattered over the ground above the fell wall which marks the upward limit of cultivation. Far below, the river throws back the sunlight, and the sound of its waters mingles with mewing of the buzzard.

River Duddon - waterfall

FARMS AND FARMING

The farms clinging to the sides of the valley above the river's flood line have a defensive look, even on a sunny day. They are dwarfed by the landscape which they punctuate, there on sufferance rather than by right, a small part of the scene rather than its dominant element. Yet the folk who have lived here over the centuries have driven the wilderness back to the fell walls, and have created green oasis where they can provide food and shelter for the sheep flocks that wander over the high fells in summertime. In the old days, a hired man, or even two, would work at each farm. Then the walls were kept in repair, and the fell gutters were kept clear, so that the rain would run off the higher slopes without creating swamps. Now the pattern has changed. One man, maybe with his son, has to manage with the help of various mechanical devices. This means that there is a greater chance of getting in the hay, for example, but there is precious little time left for labour intensive jobs like walling. The walls are a remarkable feature of Dunnerdale. They make a horizontal counterpoint to the steep and restless fellsides. They have been built with an eye to the convenience of both farmer and sheep. In addition to the gateways, fields are often connected by a stile over the wall, and an opening through it, known as a hoghole. Not that the sheep are always inclined to use the designated way. No wall yet devised by man has proved capable of penning a determined Herdwick sheep; even when reinforced by fencing along its top, or a line of barbed wire threaded along projecting posts. But when you get to know these eager little sheep you wouldn't dream of exchanging them for the great slow bumbling creatures of the soft south country.

Baskell Hall Farm

Haytiming

High Hurst

Wall and Fence

Wall patterns, Hall Dunnerdale

Preparation for showing

Autumn Gather - shepherd and flock, Hall Dunnerdale

HALL DUNNERDALE TO DUNNERDALE FOREST

Above Hall Dunnerdale the river has cut its way through Wallowbarrow Gorge. The road has to wind round the base of Wallowbarrow, through Seathwaite, where Tarn Beck joins the Duddon. Seathwaite has lost its school, but kept its pub, so that now the Newfield is the only inn in the valley. This is a wild and rocky section of the valley. Farms like Troutal seem to keep only a precarious foothold amid the stones and the trees. Much of this area has been planted by the Forestry Commission not always to the visual ruin of the landscape. On the steep slopes of Long Crag the trees soften the harsh contours of rock and scree. Seen through a thin veil of shifting rain they suggest mysterious depths and distances: in sunshine they emphasise the bold lines of the rocky outcrops between their own ragged swirls of green. Now that the quarries and mines are closed, forestry is the only industry left to back up the farming, apart from catering for the holiday makers. In Wordsworth's day the area round Seathwaite was the heart of the valley, but now many of the houses are closed for most of the year, and even important farms like Birks have only a ghost existence. It is fine for the people who practice rock climbing on the slabs above Wallowbarrow, or who tramp over the fells from a camp by the riverside, yet a sadness remains when one thinks of past days, and all the busy human life that has gone.

Rock and Rowan, Troutal

Birks Farm

Troutal

River Duddon flows through Dunnerdale Forest

Logs awaiting dispatch to the pulp-mill?

ESKDALE AND ENNERDALE HUNT

In the wild fell country at the heart of the Lake District, foxes flourish without any need of keepers to ensure a supply of victims for the hunt. As long ago as the early 17th century some of the little townships maintained a number of hounds at public expense to help in keeping foxes in check. Hunting in Dunnerdale is on foot and hence a demanding and strenuous exercise, as the pack scours the fellsides, and gives chase often over the roughest ground. Spectators drive up and down the valley in their cars, watching the action from roadside viewpoints through their binoculars. The followers keep a number of terriers with them in case the fox goes to ground in a stony barrow where the hounds cannot follow.

There is no hunt peculiar to Dunnerdale, but the Eskdale and Ennerdale pack based in the next valley regularly hunt from points along the valley. A common sight in wintertime is a group of two or three hounds which have followed a trail of the their own padding back to base, or maybe contouring round one of the slopes, noses to the ground, with no human hunt follower within miles. During the summer the hounds – great soft gentle beasts in a family circle – have a holiday in pairs usually, at one or other of the farmhouses. They will be stretched in the sunshine in a sheltered corner of the yard; or, when the show season approaches, washed and groomed, they will be seen lording it round the ring, huntsmen in full uniform in dignified attendance. The cry of the hounds and Peel's view, 'Halloo', are very much a part of life in the valley.

Edmund Porter and champion hound

Hounds and Terriers' transport

After a kill!

ROCKS AND TREES

Leaving the valley floor, the walker is soon in another, bleaker world. Above the line of the fell wall the rock becomes completely dominant. Bracken or thin coarse grass covers the ground where there is any soil at all. Here and there a tree has managed to establish itself, its shape contorted by the winds, or by the way it has grown round the boulder from which it gained some early protection. Often these trees are hollies, sparse survivors of the time when the valley was more wooded than it is today. Wordsworth tells how the shepherds would cut holly branches and strew them for their flocks to nibble. Earlier still before the sheep reigned supreme over the uplands, the mountains were forested to about the 2000' contour. There are few relics of those days in or above Dunnerdale, although on Birker Moor, up the road from the old Travellers' Rest at Ulpha, extensive remains may still be seen of the people who began the process of clearing the woodlands thousands of years ago.

There are several places along the valley sides where the rock has been exposed by the quarrymen of bygone generations. Their spoil heaps are now merging with the naturally created stony wilderness, but the remaining quarry faces show the delicate greenish colours of the natural rock, picked up by the stones which form the bed of the river far below.

Upper fellside

Holly and rock

Wind-blown holly

DUNNERDALE FOREST TO COCKLEY BECK

The final stretch of the valley floor, before the desolation of Wrynose Bottom begins at Cockley Beck, is remarkably level and fertile. The flat waste fields used to be locally noted for the quality of the wheat that they grew. Here the river is noticeably smaller but no less forceful as it rushes away from the level pastures towards Hinning House. Today Cockley Beck is the last inhabited farm. Gaitscale in Wrynose Bottom was abandoned during Wordsworth's lifetime. The roads from Cockley Beck lead on to two of the highest Lakeland passes, Hardknott, and Wrynose where Duddon has its source. These lands are even lonelier than the wide spaces of the estuary, and the farmer whose flock roams there needs more than the usual degree of strength and fortitude. He has no near neighbours. He is surrounded by the high fells. He lives in a climate that is harsh and bleak for most of the year. The snow which briefly decks the estuary grassland may remain for weeks at Cockley Beck. The sheep have to be fed by hand, then get what bite they can from those level fields in springtime. The higher in the valley you go in summer, the smaller the lambs will be; and the later the haymaking.

Our journey has brought us full circle back to Wrynose and Wordsworth's first Duddon Sonnet.

Duddon - Hinning House

Ice crystals

Dale Head Farm

Chris Akrigg dosing his flock

Chris Akrigg shearing

River Duddon and Harter Fell

Cockley Beck in winter

EPILOGUE : THE DUDDON VALLEY TODAY

Wordsworth's preferred way into the Duddon valley over Walna Scar is not the only alternative to the through route from Duddon Bridge to Cockley Beck. Even the car-bound traveller can take three other ways over the protecting hills. He may drop down from Hoses past Kiln Bank below stone walls of cyclopean masonry to join the main road at Hall Dunnerdale; he may approach from Birker Moor and plummet to the Travellers' Rest at Ulpha; or he may follow the old road from south-west Cumberland that skirts the western edge of Ulpha park.

This narrow road turns abruptly below Bigert Mire for the inevitable plunge to the valley floor. As ever in Dunnerdale, the pedestrian is at an advantage compared with the motorist. Descending slowly, he can look over the rough stone walls dividing the fields to the scattered ancient farmsteads that crouch below the wide unfriendly moor. Little dark Herdwick sheep, the wind ruffling their fleeces, are nibbling the grass with industrious relish. Cawing rooks swirl aimlessly above. On a fine autumn morning the apparent contentment of the scene recalls Wordsworth's sentiments above Seathwaite, but the low defensive aspect of the farm buildings, the ruins of barns and the wall gaps patched with rusty wire suggest rather the never-ending struggle for survival on these rainy uplands.

As our walker sets his face towards the valley, a roe deer steps delicately away from the roadside, and is lost among the hazel coppice that covers the steep slope to the rushing stream below. A little father down the road is Old Hall, possibly the original Huddlestone stronghold before Frith Hall, a romantic ruin across the fields on the right, was built. In Wordsworth's day Frith Hall was still inhabited, and Old Hall was a much more obvious ruin than it is now, tucked tidily behind a busy farm. Then, a few yards more along the road, and the main valley comes suddenly into view. Patches of sunlight illuminate the lower slopes of fells otherwise hidden by the soft grey clouds that fill the wide, windy sky. The valley fields, in various shades of green, disappear into the misty distances. The shifting cloud blurs the outlines of the fells across the river, and gives them an air of mystery. There is no way of telling just how high those hills might be. But Wordsworth-style reverie is cut short abruptly by the need to press closely to the wall to allow a big tractor and trailer to pass.

The way runs down eventually to Ulpha Bridge, past the straggling houses of the ancient settlement, and the former bobbin mill now, characteristically, converted into an attractive dwelling. On this particular November day there was no traffic other than the tractor, and the only pedestrians were a resolute middle-aged couple, balaclavas pulled down over their ears, striding up the hill. Not far beyond the Travellers' Rest one reason for this remarkable solitude became clear. Everyone was in the big field on the right of the road. Scores of sheep, invisible from the highway but easily detectable by the nose, filled a series of makeshift wooden pens fixed against the wall. They had been washed, brushed and combed to give them shining faces and fluffy fleeces; the horns double-curling from the tups' heads had been meticulously polished.

They were standing quietly in the pens, in groups of three or four; a tall, spare man wearing corduroy breeches and boots as highly polished as the horns, moved along the pens. With his long crook, he indicated a particular animal, which its owner then brought out for a closer inspection. Everything was as solemn as a cathedral service. Serious-looking groups of men and women matched the groups within the pens, only they were less smartly turned out. Most of the younger farmers were wearing shapeless jumpers and woolly hats, feet protected from the mud by battered wellies. The older men had reached an ancient jacket from the wardrobe, and they still kept a pair of boots in the kitchen to wear on special occasions. Everyone had a dog and a stick, essential for bringing a wayward ewe to the judge's call. Anyway, no shepherd feels properly dressed unless he has a dog with him.

Beyond the intent groups watching the judge's every movement, were the landrovers and pick-up trucks. Inside most of them a trail hound could be seen, waiting for the no less serious but much noisier business of the later afternoon. The presence of a number of bookies, on the far side of the inevitable beer tent, their odds chalked on blackboards, was almost disregarded for the present; but the man dragging an aniseed-soaked rag across the next field showed that soon the scene would become more animated, as the dogs were brought out and taken to the starting line. Then the sheep would be left to grind their teeth and stamp their feet with no-one to look at the bright rosettes fixed to the winner's pens.

In the small crowd waiting for the trail to start were a number of sheepskin coats, Sherlock Holmes hats and brightly coloured wellies; even a group of Chinese, especially incongruous in smart raincoats and shiny shoes, huge cameras hung at the ready round their necks. This little local gathering neatly summed up the two principal supports of the valley today – farming and tourism. The tourists have replaced the vanished industries represented by the bobbin mill and the abandoned quarry spoil heaps on the fellsides. But, like these industries, they reflect the economic situation at a particular time. They provide a very acceptable source of income, but they are marginal to the real life of the valley. The essential basis of life is still farming, as it has been from the days of the earliest settlement in the primeval forest. The farming units are larger now than they have ever been, and the farmer has more mechanical aids to lighten the drudgery of his work, but in its essential rhythms, life goes on in the way that Wordsworth knew.

Some of the old farmsteads are little changed in lay-out or appearance. The door at the front of the house, protected by a simple porch of slate slabs and seldom used, opens directly into a passage. Along the walls of this passage no end of useful farming gear is conveniently stacked. On one side of this passage is the best room, where the seventeeth century wooden bread cupboard is still in its original position along the wall. Most of these cupboards bear, amid the profusion of their carved decorations, the date of their construction and the initials of their maker, or the owner of the house (sometimes the same person).

Although the carving may be rather rustic, it makes up in vigour what it lacks in delicacy of execution. On the other side of the passage is the big living kitchen where a shining range now occupies the space formerly housing the open hearth. Little spice and salt cupboards remain in the wall alongside the fire opening, and there may well be a wooden shelf attached to two of the roof timbers for convenient storage of such household items as need to be well out of the way of cats. Behind this living room the passage takes a right-angled bend to get to the back door, opening on to the yard. The stairs rise at the end of the passage, opposite the front door, in a small extension built when the house was given a facelift between two and three hundred years ago. They turn back on themselves to give access to the separate bedrooms which replaced the cockloft reached from downstairs by a ladder.

If you were to catch him in a rare moment of inactivity, the farmer would be sitting by the kitchen fire, his stockinged feet stretched over the fender, as Wordsworth's were when he wrote the Sonnets. Instead of a manuscript, however, he is likely to be nursing a puppy dog or a favourite cat, enjoying a short after-dinner nap before beginning the next job to be done – repairing a wall gap, perhaps, or moving sheep about the fields.

His year begins in autumn when the sheep are brought down from their summer grazings on the open fell. Fat lambs go off to market; gimmer lambs which will join the breeding stock next season maybe go for a winter holiday to the lusher pastures near the coast. The remaining ewes are then put to run with the tups as the first step towards next year's lamb crop. Then the flock has to be fed and cared for through what is often a very severe winter.

When the winter weather permits, the farmer will spread muck from his beasts (now usually store cattle) on the hay meadows, layer some of his hedges, repair his walls and clean out his fell gutters so that wandering waters do not add unnecessary erosion to the list of his problems. Lambing time is late in the Duddon valley, and the nearer one approaches Cockley Beck in May, the smaller the lambs become. This is a time of year when the interests of farming and tourism may well clash. Those delightful weeks of dry weather in the spring mean that the grass is now growing, so the ewes need much more winter feed for a longer period, and the fields look as if a lawn mower had been run across them. The drier the spring, too, the later the grass can be allowed to start growing for haytiming, with the prospect of a thinner, later crop. Moreover, if the grass isn't growing in the in-bye fields, it won't be growing on the fell, either, so there will be less nourishment for the flocks when they are turned out after lambing is safely completed.

Lambing time is still the same nerve-racking 24-hours a day job that it always was. No amount of mechanisation can help here, and once it is over, the farmer cannot relax. Someone once said that every sheep's great ambition is to die, and these words can often seem gruesomely appropriate during the weeks after lambing. Finally, summer completes the cycle of the year. The flock must be given another dipping, and clipped, the hay has to be got – a tediously thankless business in a wet July – and maybe some bracken cut for winter bedding.

Relaxation for the dalesfolk has to be taken when this exacting work schedule permits an opportunity throughout the year. For most people the highlights are the shows and sports of late summer and autumn, which for the most part are still genuine local celebrations. They are great social occasions where acquaintances can be renewed, friendships strengthened or rivalries sharpened. "How are ye keeping?" ..."I clipped it when it were a twinter. It had 10 pound o' wool"..."He said he weren't comin'; he had some heifers to see to"..."Aye only for t' russlin"... The ear catches fragments of conversation like these in moving across the fields. At the same time the eye takes in the trade stands, geared to the farmyard and not the hotel or gift shop – Somebody's Sheep Dips, and Somebody Else's is way ahead in Worming. Some of the firms have contributed prizes, useful rather than glamourous – 2½ litres of disinfectant for the best animal on the field that has not won any other prize; the best wooled sheep of any age, a footrot knife.

The handicraft and produce tents contain a wonderful variety of attractive items, and, probably, a host of contributions from the local primary school pupils. These youngsters will figure largely in the fun and games which follow the serious judging of the morning session. Fell races – even a scaled-down course for tiny children – pillow fights on a greasy pole, diversions to the beer tent before the last singing competitions of the evening. Long before this the faint-hearted and the weak have fallen by the wayside. One young man is wheeling a barrow loaded with prizes and rosettes away from the field. In the car park a welly-booted leg protrudes from the side window of a landrover, along the seats of which its owner is sleeping off the afternoon's refreshment. Show days are marked with a white stone, subject for talk round the fireside for many a winter to come.

Not that the winter season is a quiet time. The regular engagements of the hunt provide a social diversion in which anyone can participate now that most people follow the hounds by car from one vantage point to the next, leaving the footslogging to the huntsman and a small band of masochistic enthusiasts. Dances, from Hunt Balls to Discos, and old-fashioned socials, often with a whist drive, provide regular diversions for the winter evenings, quite apart from the monthly round of meetings, such as the Women's Institute, in which many people are involved.

Even though today more retired persons have come to live in the valley, it is the farmers' wives who form the core of the W.I., farmers' children who are the backbone of the little school at Ulpha. The work of the farmers over millenia has shaped the landscape that we know, and is continuing to modify it, as the living community adapts to changing conditions. This landscape, together with the natural features of crag and mountain, is what the tourists flock to see. It will remain after they have gone, and in the continuity of the culture which it represents matches the symbolism of the river itself, expressed by Wordsworth in his valedictory sonnet.

LIST OF PHOTOGRAPHS